Rosie wanted a guinea-pig.

1

She wanted a spotty one.

3

She asked Mum and Dad.
Mum and Dad said, 'Yes.'

4

Mum and Rosie went
to the pet shop.

Male Rabbits

Delivery Service
Charges:
2 miles £4
Over 2 miles £6
Saturday Extra

Mind your fingers
I peck people

95p   £1.05   Jolly Drops

Special Offer

Chewy Shapes

95   £2.50

Horse Show   Sat

WWF

Wildlife Fun Run
everyone welcome

Pony Nuts   OATS

8

The spotty guinea-pig had gone.

Rosie was sad.

She took the brown guinea-pig.

She took it home.

Grandad was in the garden.

He gave Rosie a box.

To
Rosie

And Rosie had two guinea-pigs!

QED ESSENTIALS

Let's Talk

Wheels

Katie Woolley

Quarto is the authority on a wide range of topics.

Quarto educates, entertains and enriches the lives of our readers—enthusiasts and lovers of hands-on living.

www.quartoknows.com

Author: Katie Woolley
Series Editor: Joyce Bentley
Editor: Sasha Morton
Consultant: Helen Marron
Designer: Elaine Wilkinson

© 2019 Quarto Publishing plc

First published in 2019 by QED Publishing,
an imprint of The Quarto Group.
The Old Brewery, 6 Blundell Street,
London N7 9BH, United Kingdom.
T (0)20 7700 6700 F (0)20 7700 8066
www.QuartoKnows.comw

A catalogue record for this book is available from the British Library.

ISBN 978-0-7112-4435-1

MIX
Paper from responsible sources
FSC® C001701

Manufactured in Shenzhen, China PP062019

9 8 7 6 5 4 3 2 1

Photo Acknowledgments
Shutterstock: front cover Aleksandr Veremeev; back cover, p3 and 15 Ahmad Faizal Yahya; title page, p19 and 22 jambro; imprint page S-Tiden; p4-5 and 20 Ivan Kurmyshov; p6-7, 3 and 20 Dabarti CGI; p8,19 and 22 ChameleonsEye; p9 Tomasz Trojanowski; p10-11 and 20 Songquan Deng; p12-13 Oleksly Mark; p14 Valentin Valkov; p15t Kuznetsov Alexey; p16-17 Michael Gancharuk; p18l Kuznetsov Alexey; p18r Tatyana Vyc; p19bl wavebreakmedia; p19br Maciej Kopanieck; p21 Olga Sapegina; p23t Gelpi; p23l Luis Molinero; p23r SergiyN

Let's Talk

Wheels

The car has wheels.

They go round and round.

The truck has big wheels.

They go round and round.

The bike has two wheels.

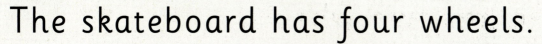
The skateboard has four wheels.

9

The red bus has four wheels too.

The train has lots of little wheels.

13

Wheels can go slow.

14

Wheels can go fast.

Zoom!

Zoom!

15

Wheels must stop too.

16

They stop in a traffic jam.

Can you count the wheels?

Match it!

Follow the line from each picture
to read the word.

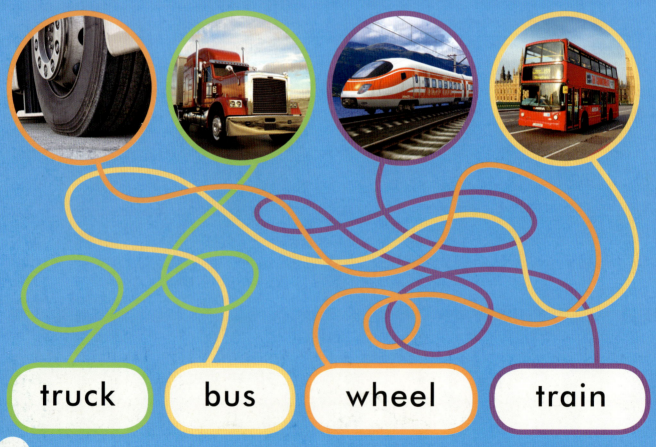

truck   bus   wheel   train

Clap it!

Say the 'Match it!' words.
Clap the syllables.

Sound it!

Sound out each of these words.

s l ow	c ar	s t o p	l o t

Say it!

Read and say these words.

of	they	go	are

Describe it!

1 Look at page 18. What do roller skates look like? What do you think it would it be like to go roller skating? Have you ever been roller skating?

2 Describe what you can see in each of these pictures. How are they the same? How are they different?

Do it!

Say a word that rhymes with **train**.

Say a word that rhymes with **go**.

Say a word that rhymes with **car**.

Look back and find!

What has lots of little wheels??

What is red and has four wheels?

Notes for Parents and Teachers

Children naturally practise their literacy skills as they discover the world around them. The topics in the **QED Essentials** series help children use these developing skills and broaden their knowledge and vocabulary. Once they have finished reading the text, encourage your child to demonstrate their understanding by having a go at the activities on pages 20–23.

Reading Tips

• Sit next to your child and let them turn the pages themselves.

• Look through the book before you start reading together. Discuss what you can see on the cover first.

• Encourage your child to use a finger to track the text as they read.

• Keep reading and talking sessions short and at a time that works for both of you. Try to make it a relaxing moment to share with your child.

• Prompt your child to use the picture clues to support their reading when they come across unfamiliar words.

• Give lots of praise as your child reads and return to the book as often as you can. Re-reading leads to greater confidence and fluency.

• Remind your child to use their letter sound knowledge to work out new words.

• Use the 'Your Turn' pages to practise reading new words and to encourage your child to talk about the text.

The red bus has four wheels too.

Colourful photographs open up further discussion points

Short, decodable sentences repeat topic words and commonly used words

Wide range of vocabulary to explore in context